indian

indian

a culinary journey of discovery

MRIDULA BALJEKAR

Love Food® is an imprint of Parragon Books Ltd

Parragon
Queen Street House
4 Queen Street
Bath BA1 1HE, UK

Copyright © Parragon Books Ltd 2007

Love Food® and the accompanying heart device is a trademark of Parragon Books Ltd

ISBN: 978-1-4054-9705-3
Printed in China

Produced by the Bridgewater Book Company Ltd

Photography: Clive Streeter
Home economists: Angela Drake and Emma Jane Frost

Notes for the Reader
This book uses imperial, metric, and US cup measurements. Follow the same units of measurement throughout; do not mix
imperial and metric. All spoon measurements are level: teaspoons are assumed to be 5 ml, and tablespoons are assumed to
be 15 ml. Unless otherwise stated, milk is assumed to be whole, eggs and individual vegetables such as potatoes are medium,
and pepper is freshly ground black pepper. Recipes using raw or very lightly cooked eggs should be avoided by infants, the
elderly, pregnant women, convalescents, and anyone suffering from an illness. Pregnant and breastfeeding women are
advised to avoid eating peanuts and peanut products. The times given are an approximate guide only.

Contents

Introduction

Spectacular natural beauty, endearing local customs, ancient cultures, and glorious food all conspire to captivate the visitor to the magical land of India, making it impossible to leave without great reluctance. The vibrant colors, exciting textures, and complex flavors of Indian cuisine, produced by the range of spices used, have made Indian food popular the world over. It is also these spices that lured a host of foreign powers to India, resulting in an exotic cuisine with a venerable history.

Cultural influences

The spice wealth of the country was recorded as early as A.D. 629 by the Chinese traveler Huien Tsang, and later by Marco Polo in 1298. Nomadic tribes, pilgrims, and traders entered the north of India and introduced their particular styles of cooking, while the western side of the country came under the influence of the ancient Persians, their contribution to Indian cuisine proving invaluable. The Portuguese ruled Goa on the west coast for four centuries and made significant contributions to the food culture of this region. The eastern belt of India, however, offers a dramatically different range of food. Here, it has absorbed the influence of Tibetan methods, together with the Anglo-Indian style of cooking introduced by the British, as well as the native Bengali cuisine. The absence of foreign influences in southern India has made this region the only one to offer a totally indigenous style of cuisine.

Regional and religious diversity

The varied geographical conditions of the country result in an equally diverse climate, which in turn dictates the types of crops grown in each region. This has had a profound influence on the cuisine of the country, and the difference in ingredients used from region to region is reflected in the variation in cooking styles. For example, it is the coconut, curry leaves, and fiery chiles locally grown in southern India that set this area's cuisine apart. In the north, the extensive use of mint, fresh cilantro, and garam masala give northern Indian food its distinctive taste and aroma. Eastern Indian cuisine has a totally different taste and flavor due to the use of mustard oil, while western Indian cuisine tends to be more dairy based, except in the princely state of Rajasthan, where exquisite game and meat dishes are prepared.

Religion has also had a significant influence on Indian cuisine. The religious taboos among the two main faiths, Hindu and Muslim, have impacted upon the culinary habits of the people. Hindus do not eat beef, as the cow is depicted as the companion of the Hindu God Krishna, and Muslims are forbidden to eat pork in their holy book, the Koran. Many Hindus are also vegetarians.

It was inevitable that a land of such varied aspects would give rise to a cuisine of essential diversity, but this diversity is nevertheless unified by one common element that lies at the heart of its cooking: the spices.

The curry craze

Indian cuisine, having been influenced and shaped into its present form by all the above factors, has now gained global recognition, and today enjoys the reputation of being one of the best in the world. As well as being diverse within the country, it has also been adapted around the world in order to incorporate local ingredients, giving rise to a fusion of colors, textures, and flavors. As well as being cooked in restaurant and home kitchens, Indian food has found its way to the supermarkets of Europe, North America, Australia, Africa, and many other countries.

Of all the different Indian dishes enjoyed around the globe, curries are probably the most well known. But what exactly is a "curry"? It is commonly believed that the word originates from a southern Indian language known as Tamil, in which "kari" simply means "a spiced sauce." It is also believed that the British anglicized this word and called it "curry."

Healthy eating

Besides offering fabulous flavors, Indian food can also be extremely healthy. The main emphasis of the Indian diet is on fresh vegetables and salads, together with rice or wheat as the staple—rice in southern India and a combination of rice and whole wheat bread in other parts of India. Meat and fish are served in smaller quantities, surrounded by inviting little side dishes. Many of the ingredients used in the cooking of these dishes are known for their medicinal properties. For instance, garlic and ginger, the two most commonly used ingredients, contain nutrients essential in fighting heart disease and combating stomach ulcers, respectively.

Essential techniques

The following ingredients and their preparation methods feature prominently in Indian cooking and the recipes in this book. Garlic and ginger, for example, are needed in almost all Indian dishes, and it is useful to have these ready prepared so that you can rustle up a dish at short notice.

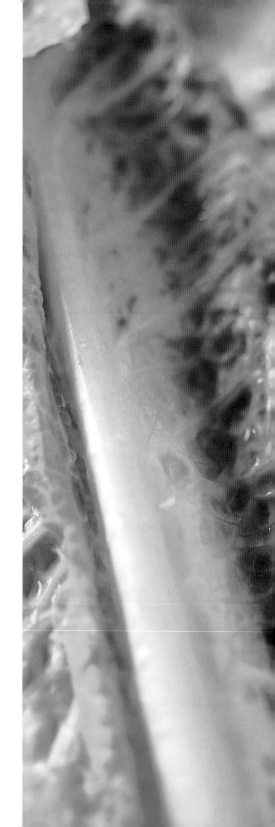

Preparing garlic purée

Peel a good quantity (at least 6 large bulbs) of garlic cloves. The easiest way to do this is to crush them lightly with the blade of a large knife—the skins will then come off easily. Put the cloves in a blender or food processor and blend to a purée, adding enough vegetable or other cooking oil to enable the blades to move. The oil will also preserve the garlic for longer. Once puréed with oil, it will keep in the refrigerator for 6 to 8 weeks, as long as you store it in an airtight container and do not allow the purée to come into contact with any moisture. Always use a clean, dry spoon to remove the required quantity of purée from the container. You can also freeze it in smaller quantities and thaw as required.

Preparing ginger purée

Use a potato peeler to peel fresh ginger or scrape the skin with a small, sharp knife. Use a cheese grater to grate the ginger, but do not use the finest side of the grater, as the ginger sticks to it. Once peeled, coarsely chop and purée with oil, as for garlic. Store in an airtight container in the refrigerator or freezer. If you buy a ready-made version, make sure it is preserved in oil and not citric acid, which tends to impair the flavor.

Preparing strained yogurt

Pour the required quantity of yogurt into a piece of cheesecloth. Gather the four corners together and tie together loosely. Put in a strainer over a bowl to allow all the liquid contents to drain. This will take 15 to 20 minutes.

How to cook perfect rice

Rice can be cooked using one of two methods: boiling and then draining, or absorption. It is the latter method that people are often concerned about using. It is a shame to boil and drain basmati rice, as its naturally fragrant, long, slender grains will not be able to retain all of its aroma and taste, so follow these simple steps for the absorption method to ensure perfect results.

It is vital to remove as much of the milling starch as possible from the rice before cooking it, so wash in several changes of cold water until the water runs clear.

Soak the washed rice in fresh cold water for about 20 minutes. This helps to remove more of the milling starch and prepares the grains to absorb the cooking liquid more efficiently, producing dry, fluffy grains. Let drain in a colander.

Once the specified amount of water is added to the rice, allow it to come to a boil and let it continue to boil for at least 2 minutes before reducing the heat to very low. A heat diffuser should be used if the heat cannot be instantly reduced to low.

Once the lid is added to the saucepan, it is most important not to lift it, as preserving the steam is vital. Cook the rice for the specified time without lifting the lid then, once cooked, let it stand for 6 to 8 minutes, with the lid on. This helps the grains to absorb any fresh starch back into themselves, which in turn prevents them sticking together.

Fluff up the rice with a fork and use a metal spoon to serve it, as the grains of exquisite basmati rice are very fragile; wooden spoons will squash the grains.

Making ghee and garam masala

Garam masala is made by combining and grinding selected spices, the recipe varying from region to region. The basic spices are known to create body heat—the word "garam" means heat and "masala" a mixture of spices. Ghee has a rich, distinctive flavor and is used liberally in Mogul food such as pilafs and kormas. There are two types of ghee: pure butterfat ghee, made from unsalted butter, and vegetable ghee, made from vegetable fat. Ghee can be heated to a high temperature without burning. Both types are available from Indian stores and larger supermarkets. Generally, pure butterfat ghee is used in Indian recipes.

Garam masala

Makes 3 1/2 oz/100 g

1/2 oz/15 g green cardamom pods
1 oz/25 g cinnamon sticks
1/4 oz/10 g cloves
1/4 oz/10 g black peppercorns
1 whole nutmeg, crushed
1/4 oz/10 g cumin seeds
1/4 oz/10 g coriander seeds

Heat a small, heavy-bottom skillet or wok over medium heat, add all the spices, and reduce the heat to low. Stir them around until you can smell their aroma; this will take no longer than a minute. Make sure that the spices do not change color; gentle heat is all that is necessary in order to activate the volatile oil in the spices.

Transfer the toasted spices to a plate and let cool, then grind in a coffee grinder or spice mill. Store the garam masala in a moisture-free, airtight container, away from direct heat.

Ghee (clarified butter)

Makes 4 oz/115 g

1 lb/450 g unsalted butter

Put the butter in a small, heavy-bottom saucepan, heat over low heat, and let melt without sizzling. Once melted, increase the heat slightly and let simmer gently for 10 to 15 minutes, during which time the milk solids will separate and the moisture will be released from the butter. A layer of foam will appear on the surface, which will then subside, indicating that the butter is now moisture free. During the entire process you will hear gentle splattering, which is the moisture in the butter that needs to dry out completely. Continue to heat the butter until the liquid is a clear golden color and the milk solids have collected at the bottom of the saucepan. Once the moisture and the milk solids are removed, the ghee is ready; the process can take up to 45 minutes, depending on the quantity of butter you are using. Let cool slightly, then strain through fine cheesecloth into a sterilized, airtight storage jar. Ghee can be stored at room temperature.

Vegetable ghee can be prepared in the same way using margarine made from vegetable oils.

Appetizers

The success of a meal depends to a large extent on how it begins, and you can be sure to tantalize the taste buds with these appetizers. Kabobs are easy to prepare and ideal for both outdoor and indoor dining, and there are several kinds to choose from here, while crisp, deep-fried Onion Bhajiyas and freshly baked Vegetable Samosas are simply irresistible.

The overall presentation of an appetizer, even for the simplest dish, is greatly enhanced if color and texture are used imaginatively. A few snipped fresh chives, finely chopped fresh cilantro leaves, and red and green chile rings can all add an inviting touch. Fresh fruits are another way of enhancing the presentation of snacks and appetizers.

Creamy chicken tikka

Murgh tikka malai

Serves 4

1 lb 9 oz/700 g skinless, boneless chicken breasts, cut into 1-inch/2.5-cm cubes

2 tbsp lemon juice

1/2 tsp salt, or to taste

1/2 cup whole milk plain yogurt, strained, or Greek-style yogurt

3 tbsp heavy cream

1 oz/25 g mild Cheddar cheese, grated

1 tbsp garlic purée

1 tbsp ginger purée

1/2 to 1 tsp chili powder

1/2 tsp ground turmeric

1/2 tsp granulated sugar

1 tbsp gram flour, sifted

1 tsp garam masala

2 tbsp sunflower or olive oil, plus 2 tbsp for brushing

3 tbsp melted butter or olive oil

salad, for serving

Mint and Spinach Chutney, for serving

There are several versions of this ever-popular dish, and this one is quite special. Grated mild Cheddar cheese and cream are added to the marinade, and the combination of the dairy ingredients has a magical effect in tenderizing the meat.

Put the chicken cubes in a nonreactive bowl and add the lemon juice and salt. Rub well into the meat. Cover and let marinate in the refrigerator for 20 to 30 minutes.

Put the yogurt in a separate nonreactive bowl and beat with a fork until smooth. Add all the remaining ingredients, except the melted butter. Beat well until the ingredients are fully incorporated. Add the chicken and mix thoroughly until fully coated with the marinade. Cover and let marinate in the refrigerator for 4 to 6 hours, or overnight. Return to room temperature before cooking.

Preheat the broiler on high for 7 to 8 minutes. Brush 6 metal skewers generously with the remaining 2 tablespoons of oil and thread on the chicken cubes. Brush any remaining marinade over the tikkas. Place the prepared skewers in a broiler pan and broil about 3 inches/7.5 cm below the heat source for 4 to 5 minutes. Brush generously with the melted butter and cook for an additional 1 to 2 minutes. Turn over and cook for 3 to 4 minutes, basting frequently with the remaining melted butter.

Balance the skewers over a large saucepan or skillet and let rest for 5 to 6 minutes before sliding the tikkas off the skewers with a table knife. Serve with salad and accompanied by the chutney.

Silky chicken kabobs

Reshmi kabob

Makes 8

¹/₃ cup raw cashews

2 tbsp light cream

1 egg

1 lb/450 g skinless, boneless chicken breasts, coarsely chopped

¹/₂ tsp salt, or to taste

2 tsp garlic purée

2 tsp ginger purée

2 green chiles, coarsely chopped (seeded if you like)

1 cup fresh cilantro, including the tender stalks, coarsely chopped

1 tsp garam masala

vegetable oil, for brushing

2 tbsp butter, melted

For serving

Mint and Spinach Chutney

mixed salad

These ground chicken breasts have a silky texture and an enticing flavor imparted by a cashew cream mixture and garam masala. The taste is subtle yet assertive, allowing you to appreciate the flavors of the different spices as well as the meat.

Put the cashews in a heatproof bowl, cover with boiling water, and let soak for 20 minutes. Drain and put in a food processor. Add the cream and egg and process the ingredients to a coarse mixture.

Add all the remaining ingredients, except the oil and melted butter, and process until smooth. Transfer to a bowl, cover, and let chill in the refrigerator for 30 minutes.

Preheat the broiler on high for 7 to 8 minutes. Brush the grid and 8 metal skewers lightly with oil. Have a bowl of cold water ready.

Divide the chilled mixture into 8 equal-size portions. Dip your hands into the bowl of cold water—this will stop the mixture sticking to your fingers when you are molding it onto the skewers. Carefully mold each portion onto the skewers, patting and stretching it gently into a 6-inch/15-cm sausage shape. Arrange the kabobs on the prepared grid and cook about 6 inches/15 cm below the heat source for 4 minutes. Brush with half the melted butter and cook for an additional 1 minute. Turn over and cook for 3 minutes. Baste with the remaining melted butter and cook for an additional 2 minutes.

Remove from the heat and let the kabobs rest for 5 minutes before sliding them off the skewers with a table knife. Serve with the chutney and a mixed salad.

Cook's tip

The kabobs can be frozen once cooked, but remove them from the heat before the stage where you baste with melted butter and cook for an additional 2 minutes. When required, defrost and place under a preheated high broiler, baste with the melted butter, and cook for 2 minutes on each side.

Tandoori chicken

Tandoori murgh

Serves 4

4 chicken pieces, about 8 oz/225 g each, skinned

juice of 1/2 lemon

1/2 tsp salt, or to taste

1/3 cup whole milk plain yogurt, strained, or Greek-style yogurt

3 tbsp heavy cream

1 tbsp gram flour

1 tbsp garlic purée

1 tbsp ginger purée

1/2 to 1 tsp chili powder

1 tsp ground coriander

1/2 tsp ground cumin

1/2 tsp garam masala

1/2 tsp ground turmeric

2 tbsp vegetable oil, for brushing

3 tbsp melted butter or olive oil

salad, for serving

lemon wedges, for garnishing

This dish from the Northwest Frontier is made with chicken on the bone. Marinated with plain yogurt as the tenderizer, along with garlic, ginger, chili, and garam masala as the spices, you can cook the chicken on a barbecue or broiler.

Make 2 to 3 small incisions in each chicken piece—this will help the flavors penetrate deeper into the meat. Put the chicken pieces in a large nonreactive bowl. Rub in the lemon juice and salt, cover, and let marinate in the refrigerator for 20 minutes.

Meanwhile, put the yogurt in a separate nonreactive bowl and add the cream and gram flour. Beat with a fork until well blended and smooth. Add all the remaining ingredients, except the oil and melted butter, and mix until the ingredients are thoroughly incorporated. Pour the mixture over the chicken and rub in well. Cover and let marinate in the refrigerator for 4 to 6 hours, or overnight. Return to room temperature before cooking.

Preheat the broiler on high for 10 minutes. Line a broiler pan with foil and brush the grid with oil. Using tongs, lift the chicken pieces out of the marinade and put on the prepared grid, reserving the remaining marinade. Cook the chicken about 5 inches/12.5 cm below the heat source for 4 minutes. Turn over and cook for an additional 4 minutes. Baste the chicken generously with the reserved marinade and cook for an additional 2 minutes on each side.

Brush the chicken with the melted butter and cook about 4 inches/10 cm below the heat source for 5 to 6 minutes, or until charred in patches. Turn over and baste with the remaining marinade. Cook for an additional 5 to 6 minutes, or until charred as before, tender, and the juices run clear when a skewer is inserted into the thickest part of the meat.

Transfer the chicken to a dish and serve with a salad and garnished with lemon wedges.

Cook's tip
This dish freezes well. Defrost completely before reheating in the center of a preheated oven at 375°F/190°C for 20 to 25 minutes, wrapped in a double thickness of foil.

Marinated lamb brochettes

Boti shashlik

Serves 4

1 lb 9 oz/700 g boned leg of lamb, cut into 1-inch/2.5-cm cubes

2 tbsp vinegar

1/2 tsp salt, or to taste

1 tbsp garlic purée

1 tbsp ginger purée

1/2 cup whole milk plain yogurt, strained, or Greek-style yogurt

1 tbsp gram flour

1 tsp ground cumin

1 tsp garam masala

1/2 to 1 tsp chili powder

1/2 tsp ground turmeric

3 tbsp olive or sunflower oil, plus 1 tbsp for brushing

1/2 red bell pepper, cut into 1-inch/2.5-cm pieces

1/2 green bell pepper, cut into 1-inch/2.5-cm pieces

8 shallots, halved

4 tbsp butter, melted

lemon wedges, for serving

Here, tender cubes of lamb are infused with a spiced yogurt marinade, skewered with red bell peppers and shallots, and broiled. The quality of the meat is of prime importance, and be sure to trim off any excess fat before cutting it into cubes.

Put the meat in a large nonreactive bowl and add the vinegar, salt, and garlic and ginger purées. Mix together thoroughly, cover, and let marinate in the refrigerator for 30 minutes.

Put the yogurt and gram flour in a separate bowl and beat together with a fork until smooth. Add the cumin, garam masala, chili powder, turmeric, and oil and mix together thoroughly. Add the yogurt mixture to the marinated meat, then add the bell peppers and shallots and stir until all the ingredients are well blended. Cover and let marinate in the refrigerator for 2 to 3 hours, or overnight. Return to room temperature before cooking.

Preheat the broiler to high. Line the broiler pan with a piece of foil. Brush the grid generously with some of the oil and brush 4 metal skewers with the remaining oil.

Thread the marinated lamb, bell peppers, and shallots alternately onto the prepared skewers. Place the skewers on the prepared grid and cook about 3 inches/7.5 cm below the heat source for 4 minutes. Brush generously with half the melted butter and cook for an additional 2 minutes. Turn over and cook for 3 to 4 minutes. Brush with the remaining butter and cook for an additional 2 minutes.

Balance the skewers over a large saucepan or skillet and let rest for 5 to 6 minutes before sliding the brochettes off the skewers with a table knife. Serve with the lemon wedges.

Kashmiri lamb chops

Tabak maaz

Serves 4

4 lamb chump chops or 8 chops

1¼ cups whole milk

1 tbsp ginger purée

½ tsp pepper

pinch of saffron threads, pounded

1½ tsp ground fennel seeds

1 tsp ground cumin

½ tsp chili powder

4 cloves

1-inch/2.5-cm piece cinnamon stick

4 green cardamom pods, bruised

1 tsp salt, or to taste

½ tsp garam masala

1 tbsp fresh mint leaves, chopped, or ½ tsp dried mint

1 tbsp chopped fresh cilantro leaves

mixed leaf salad, for serving

Deliciously spiced, succulent lamb chops make a wonderful start to a meal. You can buy fennel seeds instead of ground fennel and grind them yourself when required with a mortar and pestle or in a coffee grinder.

Remove the rind from the chops. Bring enough water to cover the chops to a boil in a medium saucepan. Add the chops, return to a boil, and cook for 2 to 3 minutes. Drain the chops, rinse, and drain again.

Put the drained chops into a large (12-inch/30-cm diameter) nonstick saucepan and add all the remaining ingredients, except the garam masala and herbs. Put the saucepan over medium heat and stir until the milk begins to bubble. Reduce the heat to low, cover, and cook for 30 minutes, turning the chops occasionally.

Remove from the heat. Using tongs, lift the chops out of the saucepan and shake the cooking liquid back into the saucepan. Strain the liquid and return to the saucepan with the chops. Cook over medium heat, turning frequently, for 7 to 8 minutes, until the liquid has evaporated and the chops are browned.

Sprinkle the garam masala evenly over the chops and add the mint and cilantro. Stir and cook for 1 minute. Serve immediately with a mixed salad.

Lamb kabobs

Gosht ke seekh

Makes 8

1/3 cup raw cashews

3 tbsp heavy cream

1 egg

1 tbsp gram flour

2 green chiles, coarsely chopped

2 shallots, coarsely chopped

1 lb/450 g fresh ground lamb

1 tsp salt, or to taste

2 tsp garlic purée

2 tsp ginger purée

1 tsp ground cumin

1 tsp garam masala

1 tbsp chopped fresh mint leaves

2 tbsp chopped fresh cilantro leaves

1/2 red bell pepper, finely chopped

4 tbsp butter, melted

2 tbsp vegetable oil, for brushing

For serving

arugula leaves, dressed with a little olive oil

Mint and Spinach Chutney

The Indian word for skewer is *seekh*. Traditionally, these kabobs are molded onto metal skewers and cooked in the Indian clay oven known as a *tandoor*. However, they lend themselves well to cooking under a gas grill or over a charcoal barbecue.

Put the cashews in a heatproof bowl, cover with boiling water, and let soak for 20 minutes. Drain and put in a food processor. Add the cream and egg and process the ingredients to a coarse mixture.

Add all the remaining ingredients, except the herbs, red bell pepper, butter, and oil, and process until thoroughly mixed. Transfer the mixture to a large bowl. Add the herbs and red bell pepper and mix well. Cover and chill in the refrigerator for 30 to 40 minutes.

Preheat the broiler on high for 10 minutes. Brush the grid and 8 metal skewers lightly with oil. Have a bowl of cold water ready.

Divide the chilled mixture into 8 equal-size portions. Dip your hands into the bowl of cold water—this will stop the mixture sticking to your fingers when you are molding it onto the skewers. Carefully mold each portion onto the skewers, patting and stretching it gently into a 6-inch/15-cm sausage shape. Arrange the kabobs on the prepared grid and cook about 6 inches/15 cm below the heat source for 4 minutes. Brush with half the melted butter and cook for an additional 1 minute. Turn over and cook for 3 minutes. Baste with the remaining melted butter and cook for an additional 2 minutes.

Remove from the heat and let the kabobs rest for 5 minutes before sliding them off the skewers with a table knife. Arrange the kabobs on a bed of the dressed arugula leaves. Serve immediately, with the Mint and Spinach Chutney.

Fish tikka

Mahi tikka

Makes 8

pinch of saffron threads, pounded

1 tbsp hot milk

1/3 cup Greek-style yogurt

1 tbsp garlic purée

1 tbsp ginger purée

1 tsp salt, or to taste

1/2 tsp granulated sugar

juice of 1/2 lemon

1/2 to 1 tsp chili powder

1/2 tsp garam masala

1 tsp ground fennel seeds

2 tsp gram flour

1 lb 10 oz/750 g salmon fillets, skinned and cut into 2-inch/5-cm cubes

3 tbsp olive oil, plus extra for brushing

lemon wedges, for serving

For garnishing

sliced tomatoes

sliced cucumber

You need a firm-fleshed fish for these delectable tikkas. Salmon has been used here, but monkfish produces an equally delicious result, although the unique characteristics of the two different fish give a distinct variation in flavor.

Soak the pounded saffron in the hot milk for 10 minutes.

Put all the remaining ingredients, except the fish and oil, in a bowl and beat with a fork or a wire whisk until smooth. Stir in the saffron and milk, mix well, and add the fish cubes. Using a metal spoon, mix gently, turning the fish around until fully coated with the marinade. Cover and let marinate in the refrigerator for 2 hours. Return to room temperature before cooking.

Preheat the broiler on high for 10 minutes. Brush the grid generously with oil and 8 metal skewers lightly with oil. Line the broiler pan with a piece of foil. Thread the fish cubes onto the prepared skewers, leaving a narrow gap between each piece. Arrange on the prepared grid and cook about 4 inches/10 cm below the heat source for 3 minutes. Brush half the 3 tablespoons of oil over the kabobs and cook for an additional 1 minute. Turn over and brush any remaining marinade over the fish. Cook for 3 minutes. Brush the remaining oil over the fish and cook for an additional 2 minutes, or until the fish is lightly charred.

Remove from the heat and let rest for 5 minutes. Serve garnished with the sliced tomato and cucumber and with lemon wedges for squeezing over.

Spicy onion fritters

Onion bhajiyas

Serves 4

heaping 1 cup gram flour

1 tsp salt, or to taste

small pinch of baking soda

1/4 cup ground rice

1 tsp fennel seeds

1 tsp cumin seeds

2 green chiles, finely chopped
(seeded if you like)

2 large onions, about 14 oz/400 g,
sliced into half-rings and separated

1 cup fresh cilantro, including the
tender stalks, finely chopped

scant 1 cup water

sunflower or olive oil,
for deep-frying

tomato or mango chutney, for
serving

These fritters are quick and easy to make, and seriously delicious. Note the spelling of bhajiya, which is the correct version, meaning a deep-fried snack, rather than the commonly used bhaji, which simply means a vegetable side dish.

Sift the gram flour into a large bowl and add the salt, baking soda, ground rice, and fennel and cumin seeds. Mix together thoroughly, then add the chiles, onions, and cilantro. Gradually pour in the water and mix until a thick batter is formed and all the other ingredients are thoroughly coated with it.

Heat enough oil for deep-frying in a wok, deep saucepan, or deep-fat fryer over medium heat to 340° to 350°F/180° to 190°C, or until a cube of bread browns in 30 seconds. If the oil is not hot enough, the bhajiyas will be soggy. Add as many small amounts (about 1/2 tablespoon) of the batter as will fit in a single layer, without overcrowding. Reduce the heat slightly and cook the bhajiyas for 8 to 10 minutes, until golden brown and crisp. Maintaining a steady temperature is important to ensure that the centers of the bhajiyas are cooked, while the outsides turn brown. Remove and drain on paper towels. Keep hot in a low oven while you cook the remaining batter.

Serve hot with a tomato or mango chutney.

Crispy vegetable triangles

Vegetable samosas

Makes 12

3 tbsp sunflower or olive oil

1/2 tsp black mustard seeds

1 tsp cumin seeds

1 tsp fennel seeds

1 onion, finely chopped

2 green chiles, finely chopped
(seeded if you like)

2 tsp ginger purée

1/2 tsp ground turmeric

1 tsp ground coriander

1 tsp ground cumin

1/2 tsp chili powder

12 oz/350 g boiled potatoes,
cut into bite-size pieces

scant 1 cup frozen peas, defrosted

1 tsp salt, or to taste

2 tbsp chopped fresh cilantro leaves

12 sheets filo dough, about
11 x 7 inches/28 x 18 cm

4 tbsp butter, melted, plus extra
for greasing

chutney, for serving

Samosas are one of the most popular snacks in India, and the original recipe is vegetarian. Traditionally, a rich dough is made at home, but filo dough is used here, which works extremely well and reduces the preparation time considerably.

Heat the oil in a saucepan over medium heat and add the mustard seeds, followed by the cumin and fennel seeds. Then add the onion, chiles, and ginger purée and cook, stirring frequently, for 5 to 6 minutes, until the onion is softened but not brown.

Add the ground spices and cook, stirring, for 1 minute. Add the potatoes, peas, and salt and stir until the vegetables are thoroughly coated with the spices. Stir in the cilantro and remove from the heat. Let cool completely.

Preheat the oven to 350°F/180°C and line a baking sheet with greased wax paper or parchment paper.

Place a sheet of filo dough on a board and brush well with the melted butter. Keep the remaining filo dough sheets covered with a moist cloth or plastic wrap. Fold the buttered filo dough sheet in half lengthwise, brush with some more melted butter, and fold lengthwise again.

Place about 1 tablespoon of the vegetable filling on the bottom right-hand corner of the filo dough sheet and fold over to form a triangle. Continue folding to the top of the sheet, maintaining the triangular shape, and moisten the ends to seal the edges. Transfer to the prepared baking sheet and brush with melted butter. Repeat with the remaining sheets of filo dough and filling.

Bake the samosas in the preheated oven just below the top shelf of the oven for 20 minutes, or until browned. Serve hot with chutney.

Savory cheese cakes

Paneer ke tikkia

Makes 8

2 large slices day- or two-day-old white bread, crusts removed

8 oz/225 g paneer, provolone cheese, or firm tofu (drained weight), grated

3 shallots, finely chopped

1 tsp fennel seeds

1/2 tsp cumin seeds

1 tbsp chopped fresh mint leaves or 1/2 tsp dried mint

2 tbsp chopped fresh cilantro leaves

1 tsp ginger purée

1/4 cup slivered almonds, lightly crushed (optional)

1 green chile, chopped (seeded if you like)

1/2 tsp garam masala

1/2 tsp chili powder (optional)

1/2 tsp salt, or to taste

1 tbsp lemon juice

1 large egg, beaten

sunflower or vegetable oil, for pan-frying

These delicious little savory cakes are made with grated Indian cheese (paneer) blended with crushed potatoes, flavored with sautéed onions, ginger, chiles, and fresh cilantro.

Soak the bread slices in a bowl of water for 1 to 2 minutes, then squeeze out all the water and crumble the slices between your palms. Put the bread in a large bowl and add all the remaining ingredients, except the oil. Mix well to form a binding consistency.

Divide the mixture in half and shape each half into 4 equal-size, flat cakes 1/4 inch/ 5 mm thick.

Pour oil into a skillet to a depth of 1 inch/ 2.5 cm and heat over medium heat. Add the cakes and cook for 5 minutes on each side, or until well browned. Drain on paper towels and serve hot.

Cook's tip
Paneer is available in large supermarkets and Asian stores, but provolone cheese or firm tofu work well as alternatives.

Main Courses

A collection of simplified classic Indian main dishes has been recreated here, including a chicken korma from Delhi enriched with pistachios, the famous slow-cooked lamb dish Rogan Josh from the foothills of the Himalayas, and a coconut-based fish curry from Goa.

Choose the leanest possible meat and follow cooking temperatures carefully. In Indian cooking, the skin of chicken is always removed to allow the spices and other flavors to penetrate. Always make sure that fish and shellfish are absolutely fresh when you buy them, and that the period of time between purchasing and cooking is as short as possible. All the dishes can be frozen—defrost in the refrigerator before reheating.

Kashmiri lamb curry

Rogan josh

Serves 4

4 tbsp sunflower or olive oil

1 large onion, coarsely chopped

2-inch/5-cm piece fresh ginger, peeled and coarsely chopped

5 large garlic cloves, coarsely chopped

14 oz/400 g canned tomatoes

3 brown cardamom pods

2 bay leaves

1 tbsp ground coriander

1 tsp ground turmeric

1 tsp chili powder

1 lb 9 oz/700 g boned leg of lamb, cut into 1-inch/2.5-cm cubes

2/3 cup plain yogurt

2 tsp gram flour

1 tsp salt, or to taste

1 tbsp tomato paste

1/2 cup warm water

1 tsp ghee or unsalted butter

1 tsp garam masala

1/2 tsp ground nutmeg

2 tbsp chopped fresh cilantro leaves

naan or plain boiled basmati rice, for serving

This deliciously spiced lamb dish from the Himalayan region is traditionally cooked with a brilliantly colored variety of chiles. This color can be replicated by mixing chili powder with Hungarian paprika and a touch of tomato paste.

Heat 2 tablespoons of the oil in a medium, heavy-bottom saucepan over medium heat. Add the onion, ginger, and garlic and cook, stirring frequently, for 5 minutes, or until lightly colored. Remove from the heat and squeeze out as much excess oil as possible from the onion mixture by pressing against the side of the saucepan. Transfer the onion mixture to a blender or food processor with the tomatoes and their juice, blend to a purée, and set aside.

Return the saucepan to low heat and add the remaining oil. Add the cardamom pods and bay leaves and let sizzle gently for 20 to 25 seconds, then add the coriander, turmeric, and chili powder. Cook, stirring, for 1 minute, then add the tomato mixture. Increase the heat to medium and continue to cook for 10 to 12 minutes, until the oil separates from the spice paste, reducing the heat to low toward the last 2 to 3 minutes.

Add the lamb and increase the heat slightly. Cook, stirring, until the meat changes color.

Put the yogurt and gram flour in a bowl and beat together with a fork or wire whisk until smooth. Reduce the heat slightly and stir the yogurt mixture, 2 tablespoons at a time, into the meat mixture. Add the salt and tomato paste. Reduce the heat to low, cover, and cook for 30 minutes, stirring occasionally.

Add the water and bring it to a slow simmer. Re-cover and cook for an additional 20 to 25 minutes, until the meat is tender.

Melt the ghee in a small saucepan over low heat, add the garam masala and nutmeg, and cook, stirring, for 30 seconds. Pour the spiced butter over the curry and stir in half the chopped fresh cilantro. Remove from the heat and serve garnished with the remaining fresh cilantro, accompanied by naan or plain boiled basmatic rice.

Lamb in fragrant spinach sauce

Saag gosht

Serves 4

1 lb 9 oz/700 g boned leg of lamb

⅓ cup whole milk plain yogurt, strained, or Greek-style yogurt

2 tbsp vinegar

2 tsp gram flour

1 tsp ground turmeric

4 tbsp sunflower or olive oil

2-inch/5-cm piece cinnamon stick, halved

5 cloves

5 green cardamom pods, bruised

2 bay leaves

1 large onion, finely chopped

2 tsp garlic purée

2 tsp ginger purée

2 tsp ground cumin

½ to 1 tsp chili powder

7 oz/200 g canned tomatoes

¾ cup warm water, plus 4 tbsp

1 tsp salt, or to taste

1 tsp sugar

9 oz/250 g spinach leaves, defrosted if frozen, chopped

2 tsp ghee or unsalted butter

1 large garlic clove, finely chopped

¼ tsp freshly grated nutmeg

1 tsp garam masala

½ cup light cream

Chile-Cilantro Naan or plain boiled basmati rice, for serving

This robust, home-style dish hails from the northern state of the Punjab, where people love good food drenched in homemade butter! Saag Gosht is traditionally eaten with bread such as naan or paratha, but it tastes equally good with rice.

Trim the excess fat from the meat and cut into 1-inch/2.5-cm cubes. Put the yogurt in a nonreactive bowl and beat with a fork or wire whisk until smooth. Add the vinegar, gram flour, and turmeric and beat again until well blended. Add the meat and mix thoroughly, cover, and let marinate in the refrigerator for 4 to 5 hours, or overnight. Return to room temperature before cooking.

Heat the oil in a medium, heavy-bottom saucepan over low heat. Add the cinnamon, cloves, cardamom pods, and bay leaves and cook gently, stirring, for 25 to 30 seconds, then add the onion. Increase the heat to medium and cook, stirring frequently, for 4 to 5 minutes, until the onion is softened and translucent. Add the garlic and ginger purées and cook for an additional 5 to 6 minutes, until the onion is a pale golden color.

Add the cumin and chili powder and cook, stirring, for 1 minute. Add the tomatoes and their juice and cook for 5 to 6 minutes, stirring frequently, then add the 4 tablespoons of warm water. Cook for an additional 3 minutes, or until the oil separates from the spice paste. Add the marinated meat, increase the heat slightly, and cook, stirring, for 5 to 6 minutes, until the meat changes color.

Add the salt and sugar, stir, then pour in the ¾ cup warm water. Bring to a boil, then reduce the heat to low, cover, and simmer, stirring occasionally, for 55 to 60 minutes.

Meanwhile, blanch the spinach in a large saucepan of boiling salted water for 2 minutes, drain, and immediately plunge into cold water.

Heat the ghee in a separate medium saucepan over low heat. Add the chopped garlic and cook, stirring, until the garlic is lightly browned. Stir in the nutmeg and garam masala. Squeeze out the excess water from the spinach, add to the spiced butter, and stir to mix thoroughly. Add the spinach mixture to the curry, then add the cream. Stir to mix well and simmer, uncovered, for 2 to 3 minutes. Remove from the heat and serve immediately with Chile-Cilantro Naan or plain boiled basmati rice.

Goan fish curry

Caldeen

Serves 4

4 skinless salmon fillets,
about 7 oz/200 g each

1 tsp salt, or to taste

1 tbsp lemon juice

3 tbsp sunflower or olive oil

1 large onion, finely chopped

2 tsp garlic purée

2 tsp ginger purée

1/2 tsp ground turmeric

1 tsp ground coriander

1/2 tsp ground cumin

1/2 to 1 tsp chili powder

heaping 1 cup canned coconut milk

2 or 3 green chiles, sliced
lengthwise (seeded if you like)

2 tbsp cider vinegar or white wine
vinegar

2 tbsp chopped fresh cilantro leaves

plain boiled basmati rice, for serving

Goa is well known for its fish and shellfish dishes, which are usually cooked in coconut milk. For this dish, salmon has been chosen because its firm flesh lends itself well to curry dishes and takes on the flavors of all the spices extremely well.

Cut each salmon fillet in half and lay on a flat surface in a single layer. Sprinkle with half the salt and the lemon juice and rub in gently. Cover and let marinate in the refrigerator for 15 to 20 minutes.

Heat the oil in a skillet over medium heat, add the onion, and cook, stirring frequently to ensure even coloring, for 8 to 9 minutes, until a pale golden color.

Add the garlic and ginger purées and cook, stirring, for 1 minute, then add the turmeric, coriander, cumin, and chili powder and cook, stirring, for 1 minute. Add the coconut milk, chiles, and vinegar, then the remaining salt, stir well, and simmer, uncovered, for 6 to 8 minutes.

Add the fish and cook gently for 5 to 6 minutes. Stir in the fresh cilantro and remove from the heat. Serve immediately with plain boiled basmati rice.

Cook's tip

This curry improves in flavor if you cook it in advance and reheat very gently before serving. You can safely store it in the refrigerator for up to 48 hours.

Pistachio chicken korma

Murgh korma pistadar

Serves 4

¾ cup shelled pistachios

scant 1 cup boiling water

good pinch of saffron threads, pounded

2 tbsp hot, whole milk

1 lb 9 oz/700 g skinless, boneless chicken breasts or thighs, cut into 1-inch/2.5-cm cubes

1 tsp salt, or to taste

½ tsp pepper

juice of ½ lemon

4 tbsp ghee or unsalted butter

6 green cardamom pods

1 large onion, finely chopped

2 tsp garlic purée

2 tsp ginger purée

1 tbsp ground coriander

½ tsp chili powder

1¼ cups whole milk plain yogurt, whisked

⅔ cup light cream

2 tbsp rose water

plain boiled rice, Lemon-Laced Basmati Rice, or naan, for serving

6 to 8 white rose petals, washed, for garnishing

It is a common misconception that korma is a mild and creamy dish. In fact, korma is not a dish but one of the several techniques used in Indian cooking. This delectable korma from Delhi has an unusual and irresistible aroma and taste.

Soak the pistachios in the boiling water in a heatproof bowl for 20 minutes. Meanwhile, soak the pounded saffron in the hot milk.

Put the chicken in a nonreactive bowl and add the salt, pepper, and lemon juice. Rub into the chicken, cover, and let marinate in the refrigerator for 30 minutes.

Melt the ghee in a medium, heavy-bottom saucepan over low heat and add the cardamom pods. When they have puffed up, add the onion and increase the heat to medium. Cook, stirring frequently, for 8 to 9 minutes, until the onion is a pale golden color.

Add the garlic and ginger purées and cook, stirring frequently, for an additional 2 to 3 minutes. Add the coriander and chili powder and cook, stirring, for 30 seconds. Add the chicken, increase the heat to medium-high, and cook, stirring continuously, for 5 to 6 minutes, until it changes color.

Reduce the heat to low and add the yogurt and the saffron and milk mixture. Bring to a slow simmer, cover, and cook for 15 minutes. Stir halfway through to ensure that it does not stick to the bottom of the pan.

Meanwhile, put the pistachios and their soaking water in a blender or food processor and process until smooth. Add to the chicken mixture, followed by the cream. Cover and simmer, stirring occasionally, for an additional 15 to 20 minutes. Stir in the rose water and remove from the heat. Garnish with the rose petals and serve immediately with plain boiled rice, Lemon-Laced Basmati Rice, or naan.

Chicken biryani

Murgh biryani

Serves 4 to 5

1/3 cup whole milk plain yogurt

1 tbsp garlic purée

1 tbsp ginger purée

1 lb 9 oz/700 g boneless chicken thighs, skinned

1 tbsp white poppy seeds

2 tsp coriander seeds

1/2 mace blade

2 bay leaves, torn into small pieces

1/2 tsp black peppercorns

1 tsp green cardamom seeds

1-inch/2.5-cm piece cinnamon stick, broken up

4 cloves

4 tbsp ghee or unsalted butter

1 large onion, finely sliced

1 1/2 tsp salt, or to taste

2 tbsp sunflower oil, for garnishing

1 onion, finely sliced, for garnishing

Cucumber in Spiced Yogurt or Vegetable Korma, for serving

Rice

pinch of saffron threads, pounded

2 tbsp hot milk

1 1/2 tsp salt

2 x 2-inch/5-cm cinnamon sticks

3 star anise

2 bay leaves, crumbled

4 cloves

4 green cardamom pods, bruised

1 lb/450 g basmati rice, washed

In this dish from the snow-fed foothills of the Himalayas, the naturally fragrant basmati rice is enhanced with cinnamon, cardamom, and star anise, and layered with delicately spiced chicken. It is cooked in a sealed pot to conserve the flavors.

Put the yogurt and garlic and ginger purées in a bowl and beat together with a fork until thoroughly blended.

Put the chicken in a nonreactive bowl, add the yogurt mixture, and mix until well blended. Cover and let marinate in the refrigerator for 2 hours.

Grind the next 8 ingredients (all the seeds and spices) in a coffee grinder to a fine powder and set aside.

In an ovenproof casserole large enough to hold the chicken and the rice together, melt the ghee over medium heat, add the onion, and cook, stirring frequently, for 8 to 10 minutes, until a medium brown color. Reduce the heat to low, add the ground ingredients, and cook, stirring, for 2 to 3 minutes. Add the marinated chicken and salt and cook, stirring, for 2 minutes. Turn off the heat and keep the chicken covered.

To make the rice, soak the pounded saffron in the hot milk and let soak for 20 minutes. Preheat the oven to 350°F/180°C.

Bring a large saucepan of water to a boil and add the salt and spices. Add the rice, return to a boil, and boil steadily for 2 minutes. Drain the rice, reserving the whole spices, and pile on top of the chicken. Dot the surface of the rice

with the saffron and milk, making sure that you add any remaining threads.

Soak a piece of wax paper large enough to cover the top of the rice fully and squeeze out the excess water. Lay on top of the rice. Soak a clean dish towel, wring out, and lay loosely on top of the wax paper. Cover the saucepan with a piece of foil. It is important to cover the rice in this way to contain all the steam inside the saucepan, as the biryani cooks entirely in the vapor created inside the saucepan. Put the lid on top and cook in the center of the preheated oven for 1 hour. Turn off the oven and let the rice stand inside for 30 minutes.

Meanwhile, heat the oil for the garnish in a small saucepan over medium heat, add the onion, and cook, stirring frequently, for 12 to 15 minutes, until well browned.

Transfer the biryani to a serving dish and garnish with the fried onions. Traditionally, biryani is eaten with Cucumber in Spiced Yogurt, but you can serve it with Vegetable Korma, if you like.

Chicken with onions

Murgh do piaza

Serves 4

1 lb 9 oz/700 g skinless, boneless chicken breasts or thighs

juice of 1/2 lemon

1 tsp salt, or to taste

5 tbsp sunflower or olive oil

2 large onions, coarsely chopped

5 large garlic cloves, coarsely chopped

1-inch/2.5-cm piece fresh ginger, coarsely chopped

2 tbsp whole milk plain yogurt

1-inch/2.5-cm piece cinnamon stick, halved

4 green cardamom pods, bruised

4 cloves

1/2 tsp black peppercorns

1/2 tsp ground turmeric

1/2 to 1 tsp chili powder

1 tsp ground coriander

4 tbsp canned crushed tomatoes

2/3 cup warm water

1/2 tsp granulated sugar

8 shallots, halved

1 tsp garam masala

2 tbsp chopped fresh cilantro leaves

1 tomato, chopped

Indian bread, for serving

The meaning of *"do piaza"* remains controversial. It is widely believed to mean a dish with twice the normal amount of onions, but connoisseurs of Mogul food argue that it is a Mogul term meaning any meat or poultry cooked with vegetables.

Cut the chicken into 1-inch/2.5-cm cubes and put in a nonreactive bowl. Add the lemon juice and half the salt and rub well into the chicken. Cover and let marinate in the refrigerator for 20 minutes.

Heat 1 tablespoon of the oil in a small saucepan over medium heat, add the onions, garlic, and ginger, and cook, stirring frequently, for 4 to 5 minutes. Remove from the heat and let cool slightly. Transfer the ingredients to a blender or food processor, add the yogurt, and blend to a purée.

Heat 3 tablespoons of the remaining oil in a medium, heavy-bottom saucepan over low heat, add the cinnamon stick, cardamom pods, cloves, and peppercorns, and cook, stirring, for 25 to 30 seconds. Add the puréed ingredients, increase the heat to medium, and cook, stirring frequently, for 5 minutes.

Add the turmeric, chili powder, and coriander and cook, stirring, for 2 minutes. Add the canned crushed tomatoes and cook, stirring, for 3 minutes. Increase the heat slightly, then add the marinated chicken and cook, stirring, until it changes color. Add the warm water, the remaining salt, and the sugar. Bring to a boil, then reduce the heat to low, cover, and cook for 10 minutes. Remove the lid and cook, uncovered, for an additional 10 minutes, or until the sauce thickens. You can adjust the consistency of the sauce to your liking by reducing or increasing the cooking time at this stage.

Meanwhile, heat the remaining 1 tablespoon of oil in a small saucepan, add the shallots, and stir-fry until browned and separated. Add the garam masala and cook, stirring, for 30 seconds. Stir the shallot mixture into the curry and simmer for 2 minutes. Stir in the fresh cilantro and chopped tomato and remove from the heat. Serve immediately with any Indian bread.

Chicken with stir-fried spices

Murgh jalfrazie

Serves 4

1 lb 9 oz/700 g skinless, boneless chicken breasts or thighs

juice of 1/2 lemon

1 tsp salt, or to taste

5 tbsp sunflower or olive oil

1 large onion, finely chopped

2 tsp garlic purée

2 tsp ginger purée

1/2 tsp ground turmeric

1 tsp ground cumin

2 tsp ground coriander

1/2 to 1 tsp chili powder

51/2 oz/150 g canned tomatoes

2/3 cup warm water

1 large garlic clove, finely chopped

1 small or 1/2 large red bell pepper, seeded and cut into 1-inch/2.5-cm pieces

1 small or 1/2 large green bell pepper, seeded and cut into 1-inch/ 2.5-cm pieces

1 tsp garam masala

Indian bread or plain boiled basmati rice, for serving

The popular jalfrazie was created during the British Raj to use up cold, cooked meat. This recipe comes from Kolkatta (previously Calcutta), where jalfrazie was served frequently to the members of the East India Company.

Cut the chicken into 1-inch/2.5-cm cubes and put in a nonreactive bowl. Add the lemon juice and half the salt and rub well into the chicken. Cover and let marinate in the refrigerator for 20 minutes.

Heat 4 tablespoons of the oil in a medium, heavy-bottom saucepan over medium heat. Add the onion and cook, stirring frequently, for 8 to 9 minutes, until lightly browned. Add the garlic and ginger purées and cook, stirring, for 3 minutes. Add the turmeric, cumin, coriander, and chili powder and cook, stirring, for 1 minute. Add the tomatoes and their juice and cook for 2 to 3 minutes, stirring frequently, until the oil separates from the spice paste.

Add the marinated chicken, increase the heat slightly, and cook, stirring, until it changes color. Add the warm water and bring to a boil. Reduce the heat, cover, and simmer for 25 minutes.

Heat the remaining 1 tablespoon of oil in a small saucepan or skillet over low heat. Add the chopped garlic and cook, stirring frequently, until browned. Add the bell peppers, increase the heat to medium, and stir-fry for 2 minutes, then stir in the garam masala. Fold the bell pepper mixture into the curry. Remove from the heat and serve immediately with Indian bread or plain boiled basmati rice.

Pork curry with chile, garlic, and vinegar

Vindaloo

Serves 4

2 to 6 dried red chiles (long slim variety), torn into 2 or 3 pieces

5 cloves

1-inch/2.5-cm piece cinnamon stick, broken up

4 cardamom pods

1/2 tsp black peppercorns

1/2 mace blade

1/4 nutmeg, lightly crushed

1 tsp cumin seeds

11/2 tsp coriander seeds

1/2 tsp fenugreek seeds

2 tsp garlic purée

1 tbsp ginger purée

3 tbsp cider vinegar or white wine vinegar

1 tbsp tamarind juice or juice of 1/2 lime

1 lb 9 oz/700 g boned leg of pork, cut into 1-inch/2.5-cm cubes

4 tbsp sunflower or olive oil, plus 2 tsp

2 large onions, finely chopped

heaping 1 cup warm water, plus 4 tbsp

1 tsp salt, or to taste

1 tsp dark brown sugar

2 large garlic cloves, finely sliced

8 to 10 curry leaves, fresh or dried

For serving

plain boiled basmati rice

vegetable side dish

The name *vindaloo* is derived from two Portuguese words: *vin*, meaning "vinegar," and *alho*, meaning "garlic." When the Portuguese traveled to India, they took pork preserved in vinegar, garlic, and pepper, which was spiced up to suit Indian tastes!

Grind the first 10 ingredients (all the spices) in a coffee grinder to a fine powder. Transfer the ground spices to a bowl and add the garlic and ginger purées, vinegar, and tamarind juice. Mix together to form a paste.

Put the pork in a large, nonreactive bowl and rub about one-quarter of the spice paste into the meat. Cover and let marinate in the refrigerator for 30 to 40 minutes.

Heat the 4 tablespoons of oil in a medium, heavy-bottom saucepan over medium heat, add the onions, and cook, stirring frequently, for 8 to 10 minutes, until lightly browned. Add the remaining spice paste and cook, stirring continuously, for 5 to 6 minutes. Add 2 tablespoons of warm water and cook until it evaporates. Repeat with the other 2 tablespoons of warm water.

Add the marinated pork and cook over medium-high heat for 5 to 6 minutes, until the meat changes color. Add the salt, sugar, and the heaping 1 cup warm water. Bring to a boil, then reduce the heat to low, cover, and simmer for 50 to 55 minutes, until the meat is tender.

Meanwhile, heat the 2 teaspoons of oil in a very small saucepan or a steel ladle over low heat. Add the sliced garlic and cook, stirring frequently, until it begins to brown. Add the curry leaves and let sizzle for 15 to 20 seconds. Stir the garlic mixture into the vindaloo. Remove from the heat and serve immediately with plain boiled basmati rice and a vegetable side dish.

Shrimp in coconut milk with chile and curry leaf

Prawn pappas

Serves 4

4 tbsp sunflower or olive oil

1/2 tsp black or brown mustard seeds

1/2 tsp fenugreek seeds

1 large onion, finely chopped

2 tsp garlic purée

2 tsp ginger purée

1 or 2 green chiles, chopped (seeded if you like)

1 tbsp ground coriander

1/2 tsp ground turmeric

1/2 tsp chili powder

1 tsp salt, or to taste

heaping 1 cup canned coconut milk

1 lb/450 g cooked peeled jumbo shrimp, thawed and drained if frozen

1 tbsp tamarind juice or juice of 1/2 lime

1/2 tsp crushed black pepper

10 to 12 curry leaves, fresh or dried

For serving

plain boiled basmati rice

vegetable side dish

This chili-hot, turmeric-tinged shrimp curry is mellowed with coconut milk and distinctively flavored with curry leaves, which are available fresh in Asian stores and dried in large supermarkets. Fresh ones can be frozen for up to three months.

Heat 3 tablespoons of the oil in a medium saucepan over medium-high heat. When hot but not smoking, add the mustard seeds, followed by the fenugreek seeds and the onion. Cook, stirring frequently, for 5 to 6 minutes until the onion is softened but not brown. Add the garlic and ginger purées and the chiles and cook, stirring frequently, for an additional 5 to 6 minutes, until the onion is a light golden color.

Add the coriander, turmeric, and chili powder and cook, stirring, for 1 minute. Add the salt and coconut milk, followed by the shrimp and tamarind juice. Bring to a slow simmer and cook, stirring occasionally, for 3 to 4 minutes.

Meanwhile, heat the remaining 1 tablespoon of oil in a very small saucepan or a steel ladle over medium heat. Add the pepper and curry leaves. Turn off the heat and let sizzle for 20 to 25 seconds, then fold the aromatic oil into the shrimp mixture. Remove from the heat and serve immediately with plain boiled basmati rice and a vegetable side dish.

Garden peas and Indian cheese in chili-tomato sauce

Mutter paneer

Serves 4

4 tbsp sunflower or olive oil

9 oz/250 g paneer, cut into
1-inch/2.5-cm cubes

4 green cardamom pods, bruised

2 bay leaves

1 onion, finely chopped

2 tsp garlic purée

2 tsp ginger purée

2 tsp ground coriander

1/2 tsp ground turmeric

1/2 to 1 tsp chili powder

5 1/2 oz/150 g canned chopped
tomatoes

scant 2 cups warm water,
plus 2 tbsp

1 tsp salt, or to taste

1 1/4 cups frozen peas

1/2 tsp garam masala

2 tbsp light cream

2 tbsp chopped fresh cilantro leaves

Chile-Cilantro Naan or other Indian
bread, for serving

Paneer, or Indian cheese, is a great source of protein for the vast majority of the Indian population who don't eat meat. This is a traditional vegetarian main course where tender morsels of paneer are simmered in a spice-infused tomato sauce.

Heat 2 tablespoons of the oil in a medium, nonstick saucepan over medium heat. Add the paneer and cook, stirring frequently, for 3 to 4 minutes, or until evenly browned. Paneer tends to splatter in hot oil, so stand slightly away from the stove. Alternatively, use a splatter screen. Remove and drain on paper towels.

Add the remaining oil to the saucepan and reduce the heat to low. Add the cardamom pods and bay leaves and let sizzle gently for 20 to 25 seconds. Add the onion, increase the heat to medium, and cook, stirring frequently, for 4 to 5 minutes, until the onion is softened. Add the garlic and ginger purées and cook, stirring frequently, for an additional 3 to 4 minutes, until the onion is a pale golden color.

Add the coriander, turmeric, and chili powder and cook, stirring, for 1 minute. Add the tomatoes and their juice and cook, stirring frequently, for 4 to 5 minutes. Add the 2 tablespoons of warm water and cook, stirring frequently, for 3 minutes, or until the oil separates from the spice paste.

Add the remaining warm water and salt. Bring to a boil, then reduce the heat to low and simmer, uncovered, for 7 to 8 minutes.

Add the paneer and peas and simmer for 5 minutes. Stir in the garam masala, cream, and fresh cilantro and remove from the heat. Serve immediately with Chile-Cilantro Naan or any other Indian bread.

Vegetable korma

Subzion ka korma

Serves 4

1/2 cup raw cashews

3/4 cup boiling water

good pinch of saffron threads, pounded

2 tbsp hot milk

1 small cauliflower, divided into 1/2-inch/1-cm florets

4 oz/115 g green beans, cut into 1-inch/2.5-cm lengths

4 oz/115 g carrots, cut into 1-inch/2.5-cm sticks

9 oz/250 g young, waxy potatoes, boiled in their skins and cooled

4 tbsp sunflower or olive oil

1 large onion, finely chopped

2 tsp ginger purée

1 or 2 green chiles, chopped (seeded if you like)

2 tsp ground coriander

1/2 tsp ground turmeric

6 tbsp warm water

1 3/4 cups good-quality vegetable stock

1/2 tsp salt, or to taste

2 tbsp light cream

2 tsp ghee or butter

1 tsp garam masala

1/4 tsp grated nutmeg

Lemon-Laced Basmati Rice, for serving

The korma style of cooking was originally used only for meat and poultry. However, its popularity is so overwhelming that various vegetarian recipes have been created in recent years. The dish is a subtle sensation of flavors and a total visual delight.

Soak the cashews in the boiling water in a heatproof bowl for 20 minutes. Meanwhile, soak the pounded saffron in the hot milk.

Blanch the vegetables, one at a time, in a saucepan of boiling salted water: blanch the cauliflower for 3 minutes, drain, and immediately plunge in cold water, blanch the green beans for 3 minutes, drain, and plunge in cold water, and blanch the carrots for 4 minutes, drain, and plunge in cold water. Peel the potatoes, if you like, and halve or quarter them according to their size.

Heat the oil in a medium, heavy-bottom saucepan over medium heat. Add the onion, ginger purée, and chiles and cook, stirring frequently, for 5 to 6 minutes, until the onion is softened. Add the coriander and turmeric and cook, stirring, for 1 minute. Add 3 tablespoons of the warm water and cook for 2 to 3 minutes. Repeat this process with the remaining warm water, then cook, stirring frequently, for 2 to 3 minutes, or until the oil separates from the spice paste.

Add the stock, saffron and milk mixture, and salt, and bring to a boil. Drain the vegetables, add to the saucepan, and return to a boil. Reduce the heat to low and simmer for 2 to 3 minutes.

Meanwhile, put the cashews and their soaking water in a food processor and process until well blended. Add to the korma, then stir in the cream. Let stand over very low heat while you prepare the final seasoning.

Melt the ghee in a very small saucepan or a steel ladle over low heat. Add the garam masala and nutmeg and let the spices sizzle gently for 20 to 25 seconds. Fold the spiced butter into the korma. Remove from the heat and serve immediately with Lemon-Laced Basmati Rice.

Cook's tip
You can store this korma in the refrigerator for 3 to 4 days, but reheat very gently, adding a little warm water at a time to maintain the consistency of the sauce.

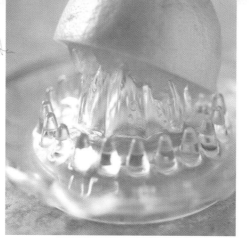

using Beans not potato Liquid, so serv on Rice

Chickpeas in coconut milk

Vatana gashi

From the palm-fringed southern coastal area of India, where coconut milk is used as an everyday stock, this is a simple but delicious dish. Traditionally, dried chickpeas would be used, but canned chickpeas are a quick and easy alternative.

Serves 4

10 oz/280 g potatoes, cut into 1/2-inch/1-cm cubes

heaping 1 cup hot water

14 oz/400 g canned chickpeas, drained and well rinsed

heaping 1 cup canned coconut milk

1 tsp salt, or to taste

2 tbsp sunflower or olive oil

4 large garlic cloves, finely chopped or crushed

2 tsp ground coriander

1/2 tsp ground turmeric

1/2 to 1 tsp chili powder

juice of 1/2 lemon

Indian bread or plain boiled basmati rice, for serving

Put the potatoes in a medium saucepan and pour in the hot water. Bring to a boil, then reduce the heat to low and cook, covered, for 6 to 7 minutes, until the potatoes are al dente. Add the chickpeas and cook, uncovered, for 3 to 4 minutes, until the potatoes are tender. Add the coconut milk and salt and bring to a slow simmer.

Meanwhile, heat the oil in a small saucepan over low heat. Add the garlic and cook, stirring frequently, until it begins to brown.

Add the coriander, turmeric, and chili powder and cook, stirring, for 25 to 30 seconds. Fold the aromatic oil into the chickpeas. Stir in the lemon juice and remove from the heat. Serve immediately with any Indian bread or plain boiled basmati rice.

Cook's tip
You can use green beans or a mixture of green beans and carrots instead of the potatoes. Black-eyed peas are also excellent for this recipe.

Side Dishes

When serving an Indian meal, the side dishes often steal the scene, since they are so varied and enticing in taste, texture, and color. Rich main courses should be teamed with simply spiced side dishes, while substantial side dishes combine well with relatively plain main courses.

Alongside classic vegetable pairings such as young, waxy potatoes with spinach and okra with onions, this section features the well-loved lentil dish Tarka Dhal, as well as Mint and Spinach Chutney—perfect with Indian snacks, and Raita, the cooling favorite. Delicately flavored Lemon-Laced Basmati Rice and different breads are also included here, and are ideal for serving with any of the main dishes in the book.

Garlic and chili-flavored potatoes with cauliflower

Aloo gobi

Serves 4

12 oz/350 g young, waxy potatoes

1 small cauliflower

2 tbsp sunflower or olive oil

1 tsp black or brown mustard seeds

1 tsp cumin seeds

5 large garlic cloves, lightly crushed, then chopped

1 or 2 green chiles, finely chopped (seeded if you like)

½ tsp ground turmeric

½ tsp salt, or to taste

2 tbsp chopped fresh cilantro leaves

Aloo gobi is a well-known and popular dish in most Indian restaurants. There are as many different versions as there are cooks. This version is easy to make, can be part-prepared ahead of time, and is simply delicious!

Cook the potatoes in their skins in a saucepan of boiling water for 20 minutes, or until tender. Drain, then soak in cold water for 30 minutes. Peel them, if you like, then halve or quarter according to their size—they should be only slightly bigger than the size of the cauliflower florets (see below).

Meanwhile, divide the cauliflower into about ½-inch/1-cm diameter florets and blanch in a large saucepan of boiling salted water for 3 minutes. Drain and plunge into iced water to prevent further cooking, then drain again.

Heat the oil in a medium saucepan over medium heat. When hot but not smoking, add the mustard seeds, then the cumin seeds.

Remove from the heat and add the garlic and chiles. Return to a low heat and cook, stirring, until the garlic has a light brown tinge.

Stir in the turmeric, followed by the cauliflower and the potatoes. Add the salt, increase the heat slightly, and cook, stirring, until the vegetables are well blended with the spices and heated through.

Stir in the cilantro, remove from the heat, and serve immediately to accompany any Indian main course dish, with rice or bread.

Potatoes with spiced spinach

Saag aloo

Serves 4

12 oz/350 g young, waxy potatoes

9 oz/250 g spinach leaves, defrosted if frozen

3 tbsp sunflower or olive oil

1 large onion, finely sliced

1 green chile, finely chopped (seeded if you like)

2 tsp garlic purée

2 tsp ginger purée

1 tsp ground coriander

1/2 tsp ground cumin

1/2 tsp chili powder

1/2 tsp ground turmeric

7 oz/200 g canned chopped tomatoes

1/2 tsp granulated sugar

1 tsp salt, or to taste

3 tbsp light cream

This traditional and popular dish is easy to make and is a perfect accompaniment to most Indian meals. Generally, fresh spinach leaves are blanched and puréed, but you can use frozen puréed spinach, which cuts down on preparation time.

Cook the potatoes in their skins in a saucepan of boiling water for 20 minutes, or until tender. Drain, then soak in cold water for 30 minutes. Peel them, if you like, then halve or quarter according to their size.

Meanwhile, blanch the spinach in a large saucepan of boiling salted water for 2 minutes, then drain. Transfer to a blender or food processor and blend to a purée. Set aside.

Heat 2 tablespoons of the oil in a medium saucepan over medium heat. Add the onion and cook, stirring frequently, for 10 to 12 minutes, until well browned, reducing the heat to low for the last 2 to 3 minutes. Remove from the heat and remove the excess oil from the onion by pressing against the side of the saucepan with a wooden spoon. Remove and drain on paper towels.

Return the pan to the heat, add the remaining oil, and heat. Add the chile and garlic and ginger purées and cook over low heat, stirring, for 2 to 3 minutes. Add the coriander, cumin, chili powder, and turmeric and cook, stirring, for 1 minute. Add the tomatoes and their juice, increase the heat to medium, and add the sugar. Cook, stirring frequently, for 5 to 6 minutes, until the tomatoes have reached a paste-like consistency.

Add the potatoes, spinach, salt, and fried onions and cook, stirring, for 2 to 3 minutes. Stir in the cream and cook for 1 minute. Remove from the heat and serve immediately with any curry.

Mushrooms in a rich tomato and onion sauce

Mushroom bhaji

Serves 4

10 oz/280 g white button mushrooms

4 tbsp sunflower or olive oil

1 onion, finely chopped

1 green chile, finely chopped (seeded if you like)

2 tsp garlic purée

1 tsp ground cumin

1 tsp ground coriander

1/2 tsp chili powder

1/2 tsp salt, or to taste

1 tbsp tomato paste

3 tbsp water

1 tbsp snipped fresh chives, for garnishing

Mushroom bhaji is not a traditional Indian dish, but mushrooms do seem to have a certain affinity with a spiced, tomato-based sauce. It is important to choose the right combination of spices in order to complement the natural taste of the mushrooms.

Wipe the mushrooms with damp paper towels and thickly slice.

Heat the oil in a medium saucepan over medium heat. Add the onion and chile and cook, stirring, for 5 to 6 minutes, until the onion is softened but not brown. Add the garlic purée and cook, stirring, for 2 minutes.

Add the cumin, coriander, and chili powder and cook, stirring, for 1 minute. Add the mushrooms, salt, and tomato paste and stir until all the ingredients are blended.

Sprinkle the water evenly over the mushrooms and reduce the heat to low. Cover and cook for 10 minutes, stirring halfway through. The sauce should have thickened, but if it appears runny, cook, uncovered, for 3 to 4 minutes, or until you achieve the desired consistency.

Transfer to a serving dish, sprinkle the chives on top, and serve immediately.

Okra stir-fried with onions

Bhindi-piaz

Serves 4

10 oz/280 g okra

1 small red bell pepper

1 onion

2 tbsp sunflower or olive oil

1 tsp black or brown mustard seeds

1/2 tsp cumin seeds

3 large garlic cloves, lightly crushed, then chopped

1/2 tsp chili powder

1/2 tsp salt, or to taste

1/2 tsp garam masala

plain boiled basmati rice, for serving

Okra stir-fried with onions and spices makes a superb side dish. Here, the combination of the soft green okra, bright red bell pepper, and white onion, all dotted with black mustard seeds, creates a colorful, appetizing effect.

Scrub each okra gently, rinse well in cold running water, then slice off the hard head. Halve diagonally and set aside.

Remove the seeds and core from the red bell pepper and cut into 11/2-inch/4-cm strips. Halve the onion lengthwise and cut into 1/4-inch/5-mm thick slices.

Heat the oil in a heavy-bottom skillet or wok over medium heat. When hot but not smoking, add the mustard seeds, followed by the cumin seeds. Remove from the heat and add the garlic. Return to low heat and cook the garlic gently, stirring, for 1 minute, or until lightly browned.

Add the okra, red bell pepper, and onion, increase the heat to medium-high, and stir-fry for 2 minutes. Add the chili powder and salt and stir-fry for an additional 3 minutes. Add the garam masala and stir-fry for 1 minute. Remove from the heat and serve immediately with plain boiled basmati rice.

Cook's tip

Make sure that the oil is at the right temperature or else the mustard seeds will not release their delightful nutty taste. To test the temperature, drop 1 or 2 mustard seeds into the hot oil—if they pop straight away, the oil is just right.

Lentils with cumin and shallots

Tarka dhal

The word *tarka* means "tempering." Tarka dhal is easy to cook, as the boiled dhal is simply tempered with a few whole spices, and either onion (or in this case shallot) or garlic is added to the hot oil before being folded into the cooked lentils.

Serves 4

1 cup red lentils

3 1/2 cups water

1 tsp salt, or to taste

2 tsp sunflower or olive oil

1/2 tsp black or brown mustard seeds

1/2 tsp cumin seeds

4 shallots, finely chopped

2 green chiles, chopped (seeded if you like)

1 tsp ground turmeric

1 tsp ground cumin

1 fresh tomato, chopped

2 tbsp chopped fresh cilantro leaves

Lemon-Laced Basmati Rice or naan, for serving

Wash the lentils until the water runs clear and put into a medium saucepan. Add the water and bring to a boil. Reduce the heat to medium and skim off the froth. Cook, uncovered, for 10 minutes. Reduce the heat to low, cover, and cook for 45 minutes, stirring occasionally to ensure that the lentils do not stick to the bottom of the pan as they thicken. Stir in the salt.

Meanwhile, heat the oil in a small saucepan over medium heat. When hot but not smoking, add the mustard seeds, followed by the cumin seeds. Add the shallots and chiles and cook, stirring, for 2 to 3 minutes, then add the turmeric and ground cumin. Add the tomato and cook, stirring, for 30 seconds.

Fold the shallot mixture into the cooked lentils. Stir in the cilantro, remove from the heat, and serve immediately with Lemon-Laced Basmati Rice or naan.

Cook's tip
If you add salt too soon to the lentils, they will take longer to cook.

Cucumber in spiced yogurt

Kheeva ka raita

Serves 4 to 5

1 small cucumber

3/4 cup whole milk plain yogurt

1/4 tsp granulated sugar

1/4 tsp salt

1 tsp cumin seeds

10 to 12 black peppercorns

1/4 tsp paprika

mixed vegetable curry, for serving

Raita is a generic name for any salad with a spiced yogurt dressing. In the north of India, the yogurt is flavored with roasted crushed cumin seeds and chile, while southern India excels in making a yogurt dressing with a hot oil seasoning.

Peel the cucumber and scoop out the seeds. Cut the flesh into bite-size pieces and set aside.

Put the yogurt in a bowl and beat with a fork until smooth. Add the sugar and salt and mix well.

Preheat a small, heavy-bottom saucepan over medium-high heat. When the pan is hot, turn off the heat and add the cumin seeds and peppercorns. Stir around for 40 to 50 seconds, until they release their aroma. Remove from the pan and let cool for 5 minutes, then crush in a mortar with a pestle or on a hard surface with a rolling pin.

Set aside 1/4 teaspoon of this mixture and stir the remainder into the yogurt. Add the cucumber and stir to mix.

Transfer the raita to a serving dish and sprinkle with the reserved toasted spices and the paprika.

Cook's tip

To add an extra dimension to the taste and texture of the raita, crush 1/3 cup roasted salted peanuts. Mix half into the raita and sprinkle the remainder on top just before serving.

Mint and spinach chutney

Pudina-palak ki chutney

Serves 4 to 6

2 oz/55 g tender fresh spinach leaves

3 tbsp fresh mint leaves

2 tbsp chopped fresh cilantro leaves

1 small red onion, coarsely chopped

1 small garlic clove, chopped

1 green chile, chopped (seeded if you like)

2$\frac{1}{2}$ tsp granulated sugar

1 tbsp tamarind juice or juice of $\frac{1}{2}$ lemon

Chutneys and raitas are an integral part of an Indian meal. Snacks and appetizers such as samosas, onion bhajiyas, and tikkas are always accompanied by an array of mouthwatering chutneys. This chutney tastes wonderful, yet it is so simple to make.

Put all the ingredients in a blender or food processor and blend until smooth, adding only as much water as necessary to enable the blades to move.

Transfer to a serving bowl, cover, and chill in the refrigerator for at least 30 minutes.

Cook's tip

If you like the refreshing mint and cilantro dip served in Indian restaurants, mix a tablespoonful of this chutney with $\frac{1}{2}$ cup whole milk plain yogurt. Taste and adjust the seasoning if necessary.

Mint and cilantro rice with toasted pine nuts

Pudina-dhania ka chawal

Serves 4

good pinch of saffron threads, pounded

2 tbsp hot milk

heaping 1 cup basmati rice

2 tbsp sunflower or olive oil

2-inch/5-cm piece cinnamon stick, broken in half

4 green cardamom pods, bruised

2 star anise

2 bay leaves

2 cups lukewarm water

3 tbsp fresh cilantro leaves, finely chopped

2 tbsp fresh mint leaves, finely chopped, or 1 tsp dried mint

1 tsp salt, or to taste

scant 1/4 cup pine nuts

The slender grains of fragrant basmati rice complement the delicately flavored pine nuts, both prized ingredients from northern India, in this sumptuous pilaf. Saffron adds an exotic touch, with its age-old reputation for being rare and costly.

Soak the pounded saffron threads in the hot milk and set aside until you are ready to use.

Wash the rice in several changes of cold water until the water runs clear. Let soak in fresh cold water for 20 minutes, then let drain in a colander.

Heat the oil in a medium, heavy-bottom saucepan over low heat. Add the cinnamon, cardamom, star anise, and bay leaves and let sizzle gently for 20 to 25 seconds. Add the rice and stir well to ensure that the grains are coated with the flavored oil.

Add the water, stir once, and bring to a boil. Add the saffron and milk, cilantro, mint, and salt and boil for 2 to 3 minutes. Cover tightly, reduce the heat to very low, and cook for 7 to 8 minutes. Turn off the heat and let stand, covered, for 7 to 8 minutes.

Meanwhile, preheat a small, heavy-bottom skillet over medium heat, add the pine nuts, and cook, stirring, until they begin to glisten with their natural oils and are lightly toasted. Alternatively, cook in a foil-covered broiler pan under a preheated medium broiler, turning 2 to 3 times, until lightly toasted. Transfer to a plate and let cool.

Add half the toasted pine nuts to the rice and fluff up the rice with a fork. Transfer to a serving dish, garnish with the remaining pine nuts, and serve immediately.

Lemon-laced basmati rice

Nimbu chawal

Serves 4

heaping 1 cup basmati rice

2 tbsp sunflower or olive oil

1/2 tsp black or brown mustard seeds

10 to 12 curry leaves, preferably fresh

scant 1/4 cup cashews

1/4 tsp ground turmeric

1 tsp salt, or to taste

2 cups hot water

2 tbsp lemon juice

1 tbsp snipped fresh chives, for garnishing

In this much-loved dish from southern India, the snow-white grains of basmati rice are tinged with turmeric and adorned with black mustard seeds. The main flavor here is that of curry leaves, which is the hallmark of southern Indian cuisine.

Wash the rice in several changes of cold water until the water runs clear. Let soak in fresh cold water for 20 minutes, then let drain in a colander.

Heat the oil in a nonstick saucepan over medium heat. When hot but not smoking, add the mustard seeds, followed by the curry leaves and the cashews (in that order).

Stir in the turmeric, quickly followed by the rice and salt. Cook, stirring, for 1 minute, then add the hot water and lemon juice. Stir once, bring to a boil, and boil for 2 minutes. Cover tightly,

reduce the heat to very low, and cook for 8 minutes. Turn off the heat and let stand, covered, for 6 to 7 minutes. Fork through the rice and transfer to a serving dish. Garnish with the chives and serve immediately.

Cook's tip

It is important to allow the cooked rice to stand to enable the grains to absorb any remaining moisture. Use a metal spoon to transfer the rice to the serving dish, as a wooden spoon will squash the delicate grains.

Griddle-roasted flat bread

Chapatti

Makes 16

scant 3 cups chapatti flour (atta), plus extra for dusting

1 tsp salt

½ tsp granulated sugar

2 tbsp sunflower or olive oil

heaping 1 cup lukewarm water

In Indian homes, chapattis are made every day, using a flour known as *atta*. Asian stores sell atta, but you can substitute whole wheat bread flour combined with all-purpose flour, at a ratio of two-thirds whole wheat to one-third all-purpose.

Mix the chapatti flour, salt, and sugar together in a large bowl. Add the oil and work well into the flour mixture with your fingertips. Gradually add the water, mixing at the same time. When the dough is formed, transfer to a counter, and knead for 4 to 5 minutes. The dough is ready when all the excess moisture is absorbed by the flour. Alternatively, mix the dough in a food processor. Wrap the dough in plastic wrap and let rest for 30 minutes.

Divide the dough in half, then cut each half into 8 equal-size pieces. Form each piece into a ball and flatten into a round cake. Dust each cake lightly in the flour and roll out to a 6-inch/15-cm round. Keep the remaining cakes covered while you are working on one. The chapattis will cook better when freshly rolled out, so roll out and cook one at a time.

Preheat a heavy-bottom cast-iron griddle (tawa) or a large, heavy-bottom skillet over medium-high heat. Put a chapatti on the griddle and cook for 30 seconds. Using a thin spatula, turn over and cook until bubbles begin to appear on the surface. Turn over again. Press the edges down gently with a clean cloth to encourage the chapatti to puff up—they will not always puff up, but this doesn't matter. Cook until brown patches appear on the underside. Remove from the pan and keep hot by wrapping in a piece of foil lined with paper towels. Repeat with the remaining dough cakes.

Chile-cilantro naan

Mirch-dhania ke naan

Makes 8

3¹/₄ cups all-purpose flour

2 tsp sugar

1 tsp salt

1 tsp baking powder

1 egg

heaping 1 cup milk

2 tbsp sunflower or olive oil, plus extra for oiling

2 fresh red chiles, chopped (seeded if you like)

1 cup fresh cilantro leaves, chopped

2 tbsp butter, melted

Naan came to India with the ancient Persians, and it means "bread" in their language. Naan is traditionally made in the *tandoor* (Indian clay oven), but this can be emulated by using a very hot broiler.

Sift the flour, sugar, salt, and baking powder together into a large bowl. Whisk the egg and milk together and gradually add to the flour, mixing it with a wooden spoon, until a dough is formed.

Transfer the dough to a counter, make a depression in the center of the dough, and add the oil. Knead for 3 to 4 minutes, until the oil is absorbed by the flour and you have a smooth and pliable dough. Wrap the dough in plastic wrap and let rest for 1 hour.

Divide the dough into 8 equal-size pieces, form each piece into a ball, and flatten into a thick cake. Cover the dough cakes with plastic wrap and let rest for 10 to 15 minutes.

Preheat the broiler on high for 10 minutes, line a broiler pan with a piece of foil, and brush with oil.

The traditional shape of naan is teardrop, but you can make them any shape you wish. To make the traditional shape, roll each flattened cake into a 5-inch/13-cm diameter round and pull the lower end gently. Carefully roll out again, maintaining the teardrop shape, to about 9 inches/23 cm in diameter. Alternatively, roll the flattened cakes out to 9-inch/23-cm rounds.

Mix the chiles and cilantro together, then divide into 8 equal portions and spread each on the surface of a naan. Press gently so that the mixture sticks to the dough. Transfer a naan to the prepared broiler pan and cook 5 inches/12.5 cm below the heat source for 1 minute, or until slightly puffed and brown patches appear on the surface. Watch carefully, and as soon as brown spots appear on the surface, turn over and cook the other side for 45 to 50 seconds, until lightly browned. Remove from the broiler and brush with the melted butter. Wrap in a dish towel while you cook the remaining naans.

Desserts

Serving an elaborate dessert is not an everyday practice in India. Fresh fruits are a popular way to end a meal, their fresh, tangy flavors offering a refreshing contrast to the spiciness of the previous courses. However, India does have a dazzling variety of sweets and desserts that are reserved for special occasions, and these differ from region to region.

A selection of the most popular Indian desserts are featured in this section, such as the sumptuous iced kulfi flavored with mango; a creamy rice dish perfumed with rose water and cardamom; and a rich fudge-like candy made from carrots cooked in milk and enriched with nuts. As with an appetizer, choose a dessert that complements the main course.

Mango-flavored iced dessert

Aam ki kulfi

Serves 6 to 8

heapin 1 1/2 cups canned evaporated milk

1 1/4 cups light cream

1/4 cup ground almonds

1/2 to 1/3 cup granulated sugar

1 lb/450 g mango purée

1 tsp freshly ground cardamom seeds

scant 1/4 cup shelled unsalted pistachios, for decorating

Kulfi is a dairy-based dessert flavored with fruits and nuts. Traditionally, it is made by reducing a large volume of milk to the consistency of condensed milk. This recipe is less labor-intensive, using evaporated milk and light cream.

Pour the evaporated milk and cream into a heavy-bottom saucepan and stir to mix. Put over medium heat. Mix the ground almonds and sugar together, then add to the milk mixture. Cook, stirring, for 6 to 8 minutes, until the mixture thickens slightly.

Remove from the heat and let the mixture cool completely, stirring from time to time to prevent a skin forming. When completely cold, stir in the mango purée and ground cardamom.

Meanwhile, preheat a small saucepan over medium heat, add the pistachios, and toast for 2 to 3 minutes. Let cool, then lightly crush. Store in an airtight container until required.

Kulfi is set in traditional conical-shaped plastic or steel molds, which you can buy from Asian stores, but you can use decorative individual molds or ice lolly molds instead. Fill the containers of your choice with the kulfi mixture and freeze for 5 to 6 hours. Traditional molds hold about 2 tablespoons of the kulfi mixture, but you can use larger containers if you like. Transfer the kulfi to the refrigerator for 40 minutes, then cut into portions with a sharp knife. Serve sprinkled with the crushed pistachios to decorate.

Cook's tip
Brush the bottom of the saucepan with a little melted butter or oil before mixing the milk and cream. This prevents the mixture from sticking.

Indian rice dessert

Firni

Serves 4

good pinch of saffron threads, pounded

2 tbsp hot milk

3 tbsp ghee or unsalted butter

heaping ¹/₂ cup ground rice

¹/₄ cup slivered almonds

scant ¹/₄ cup seedless raisins

2¹/₂ cups whole milk

2 cups evaporated milk

¹/₄ cup superfine sugar

12 plumped dried apricots, sliced

1 tsp freshly ground cardamom seeds

¹/₂ tsp freshly grated nutmeg

2 tbsp rose water

For decorating

¹/₄ cup walnut pieces

2 tbsp shelled unsalted pistachios

This is a hugely popular north Indian dessert, where ground rice is cooked in thickened milk with apricots, seedless raisins, almonds, and pistachios, with the exotic aroma of rose water and cardamom. It is best served chilled.

Place the pounded saffron in the hot milk and let soak until needed.

Set aside 2 teaspoons of the ghee and melt the remainder in a heavy-bottom saucepan over low heat. Add the ground rice, almonds, and raisins and cook, stirring, for 2 minutes. Add the whole milk, increase the heat to medium, and cook, stirring, until it begins to bubble gently. Reduce the heat to low and cook, stirring frequently, for 10 to 12 minutes, to prevent the mixture sticking to the bottom of the pan.

Add the evaporated milk, sugar, and apricots, setting a few slices aside to decorate. Cook, stirring, until the mixture thickens to the consistency of a pouring custard.

Add the reserved saffron and milk mixture, cardamom, nutmeg, and rose water, stir to distribute well, and remove from the heat. Let cool, then cover and chill in the refrigerator for at least 2 hours.

Melt the reserved ghee in a small saucepan over low heat. Add the walnuts and cook, stirring, until they brown a little. Remove and drain on paper towels. Brown the pistachios in the remaining ghee in the saucepan, remove, and drain on paper towels. Let the pistachios cool, then lightly crush.

Serve the dessert decorated with the fried nuts and the reserved apricot slices.

Soft carrot fudge

Gajjar ka halwa

Serves 4 to 6

4 tbsp ghee or unsalted butter

1-inch/2.5-cm piece cinnamon stick, halved

1/4 cup slivered almonds

scant 1/4 cup cashews

scant 1/4 cup seedless raisins

1 lb/450 g grated carrots

2 1/2 cups whole milk

scant 3/4 cup superfine sugar

1/2 tsp freshly ground cardamom seeds

1/2 tsp freshly grated nutmeg

1/4 cup heavy cream

2 tbsp rose water

vanilla ice cream or whipped heavy cream, for serving

This delicious dessert is made by cooking grated carrots in thickened milk to a soft, fudge-like consistency. A variety of contrasts in taste and texture are created by adding raisins, mixed nuts, cardamom, nutmeg, and rose water.

Melt the ghee in a heavy-bottom saucepan over low heat. Add the cinnamon stick and let sizzle gently for 25 to 30 seconds. Add the almonds and cashews and cook, stirring, until lightly browned. Remove about a dessertspoon of the nuts and set aside.

Add the raisins, carrots, milk, and sugar to the saucepan, increase the heat to medium, and bring the milk to boiling point. Continue to cook over low-medium heat for 15 to 20 minutes, until the milk evaporates completely, stirring frequently, and scraping and blending in any thickened milk that sticks to the side of the saucepan. Don't allow any milk that is stuck to the side to brown or burn, as this will give the dessert an unpleasant flavor.

Stir in the cardamom, nutmeg, cream, and rose water. Remove from the heat and let cool slightly, then serve topped with a scoop of vanilla ice cream or whipped heavy cream. Sprinkle the reserved nuts on top of the ice cream or cream, to decorate.

Sweet saffron rice with caramelized pineapple

Ananas ka muzzafar

Serves 4 to 6

good pinch of saffron threads, pounded

2 tbsp hot milk

scant 1 cup basmati rice

1/2 fresh pineapple (8 oz/225 g prepared weight)

4 tbsp ghee or unsalted butter

3/4–scant 1 cup superfine sugar

4 green cardamom pods, bruised

4 cloves

2 x 1/2-inch/1-cm pieces cinnamon stick

1 1/4 cups warm water

melted butter or vegetable oil, for brushing

1/3 cup seedless raisins

scant 1/4 cup toasted slivered almonds, for decorating

light cream, for serving

The exotic perfume and delicious golden flesh of pineapple, combined with the seductive fragrance and the slender, silky grains of basmati rice bathed in the evocative richness of saffron—this is ambrosia in all its glory!

Preheat the oven to 325°F/160°C. Soak the pounded saffron in the hot milk.

Wash the rice in several changes of cold water, then let drain in a colander.

Peel the pineapple and remove the "eyes" with a small, sharp knife. Cut the flesh into bite-size pieces.

Melt 1 tablespoon of the ghee in a large, heavy-bottom skillet over low heat. Add the pineapple, sprinkle with 2 tablespoons of the sugar, and increase the heat to high. Cook, stirring, for 3 to 4 minutes, or until the pineapple begins to caramelize a little, then remove from the heat.

Melt the remaining ghee in a heavy-bottom saucepan over low heat. Add the cardamom pods, cloves, and cinnamon stick and cook, stirring, for 25 to 30 seconds. Add the rice, increase the heat slightly, and cook, stirring, for 2 to 3 minutes. Add the saffron and milk and the warm water, bring to a boil, and boil for 2 minutes, then reduce the heat to low. Cook, uncovered, for 2 to 3 minutes, until the surface liquid has been absorbed by the grains. Remove from the heat.

Brush the sides and the base of a lidded ovenproof dish with a little butter and add one-third of the rice. Top with one-third of the raisins, followed by one-third of the pineapple pieces. Sprinkle over one-third of the remaining sugar evenly. Repeat this process twice more, ensuring that you finish with a layer of raisins, pineapple, and sugar.

Soak a piece of wax paper, crumple it, then place loosely over the top layer of fruit and sugar. Cover with a piece of foil and seal the edges by pressing it around the entire rim. Put the lid on and bake in the center of the preheated oven for 35 to 40 minutes. Turn off the oven and let the rice stand inside for 10 to 15 minutes.

Decorate with the slivered almonds and serve hot or cold with cream.

Ginger ice cream with date and tamarind sauce

Adrak, khajur aur imli ice cream

Serves 4 to 5

Ice cream

4 cups carton vanilla ice cream

2 tsp ground ginger

Tamarind sauce

1/3 cup seedless raisins

1/2 cup pitted dried dates

heaping 1 cup boiling water

2 rounded tsp tamarind concentrate or 3 tbsp tamarind juice

scant 1/4 cup molasses sugar

7 oz/200 g candied ginger, chopped, for serving

This is a cheat's version of a delicious and exotic Indian dessert, made with store-bought vanilla ice cream blended with ground ginger and served with a tangy tamarind sauce. It provides the perfect way to finish a spicy meal.

Let the ice cream stand at room temperature for 35 to 40 minutes to soften, then transfer to a bowl. Add the ground ginger and beat well. Return the mixture to the carton and freeze for 3 to 4 hours.

Meanwhile, to make the sauce, put the raisins and dates in a heatproof bowl, pour over the boiling water, and let soak for 15 to 20 minutes.

Transfer to a food processor, add the tamarind and sugar, and blend to a smooth purée. Transfer to a nonreactive bowl and let cool.

Put scoops of the ice cream into stemmed glasses and drizzle over the sauce. Arrange 1 dessertspoon of candied ginger on top of each dessert and serve immediately. Serve any extra sauce separately.

Index